To Rober

THE POPES
from St Peter to John Paul II

Revised by

BRENDAN WALSH

LONDON

CATHOLIC TRUTH SOCIETY

PUBLISHERS TO THE HOLY SEE

The authorities for the lists of the early Popes are as follows;

St Irenæus (Bishop of Lyons in the first half of the second century) gives the names, but not the lengths of the reigns, up to St Eleutherius.

Eusebius (the historian, to whom we owe the greater part of our knowledge of the first three centuries of the Church) gives both names and dates up to St Marcellinus.

An unknown Chronologist gives a list up to Liberius.

St Jerome includes St Damasus, of whom he was the secretary.

The "Liber Pontificalis" continues the Chronologist's list up to the end of the Middle Ages (Martin V) but is sometimes inaccurate as to the dates of events.

The dates of the earliest Popes, up to St Victor I, are very uncertain. After that time they are tolerably reliable.

In the general persecution started by Decius (249-251) a special feature was the destruction of "the sacred books of the Christians". Not only were manuscripts of the Scriptures thus destroyed but much also, including calendars, martyrologies, liturgical documents and other records. This campaign was renewed and intensified in the great final persecution initiated by Galerius in the year 303. That is why Christians who saved their lives by *handing over* documents were called *traditores*.

The names of anti-popes are given in square brackets.

THE POPES

St Peter. From the Gospel we learn that Our Lord placed him over the whole Church. The Acts give the events of his ministry in Palestine. He passed some time in Antioch in Syria. It is also probable that he preached the Gospel in the greater part of what we now call Asia Minor. It is historically certain that he came to Rome. The House of Hermes, excavated on the Via Appia in 1915, contains many inscriptions showing that he used the house for his ministry. He was put to death in Rome under Nero (? 64 or 67).

St Linus (67 – 76; Tuscan). Mentioned in the first Eucharistic Prayer of the Mass he may be the disciple of whom St Paul —writing to St Timothy from Rome— makes mention (II Timothy iv. 21).

St Cletus (or Anacletus) (76 – 88 ; Roman). St Jerome calls him sometimes by one name, sometimes by the other. A few old documents, by mistake, took them for two separate Popes.

St Clement (88 – 97; Roman). A celebrated Epistle of his is still extant. Its date may be put at about 96, and it is one of the oldest evidences for the Primacy of the Roman See. According to St Irenæus, he " had seen and conversed with the Blessed Apostles ".

St Evaristus (c. 97 – c. 105; Greek).

St Alexander I (105 – 115; Roman).

St Sixtus I (115 – 125; Roman).

St Telesphorus (125 – 136; Greek). Like all his predecessors he was, according to both St Irenæus and Eusebius, a martyr.

St Hyginus (136 – 140; Greek).

St Pius I (140 – 155; Italian of Aquileia). According to the ' Fragment of Muratori ', and the *Liber Pontificalis*, this Pope was the brother of Hermas the writer, author of *The Shepherd*. During this reign, Gnosticism (a complicated heresy which considered matter as evil) gave trouble to the Church; St Justin, martyr, an important writer, flourished.

St Anicetus (155 – 166; Syrian). St Polycarp (disciple of St John the Evangelist) came to Rome (160 – 162) to discuss the date of Easter. The question could not then be settled: " Polycarp could not persuade the Pope, nor the Pope, Polycarp."

St Soter (166 – 175; Greek). Eusebius, quoting Denys of Corinth, makes this Pope author of an Epistle to the Corinthians.

St Eleutherius (175 – 189; Greek), was visited, about 177, by St Irenæus, later Bishop of Lyons.

St Victor I (189 – 199; African) emphatically affirmed the Primacy of the Roman See, notably in the question of the date of Easter. He opposed the Gnostic (see St Pius I) and Monarchian heresies (the last a heresy about the Blessed Trinity).

St Zephyrinus (199 – 217; Roman) also opposed the Monarchian heresy, and condemned the Montanists—a revivalist movement that developed into a sect apart.

St Calixtus I (217 – 222); Roman). As a deacon he was administrator of the catacomb on the Appian Way which bears his name. As Pope he greatly modified the severe penitential discipline in use in the first age of the

Church. For this Tertullian and Hippolytus expostulated violently with him and even created a schism. He decreed the Ember Days.

[S. Hippolytus, the first anti-pope.]

St Urban I (222 – 230; Roman).

St Pontian (230 – 235; Roman) approved of the condemnation of Origen by Demetrius, Bishop of Alexandria. This Pope was banished to Sardinia, and there died of the ill-treatment he received.

St Anteros (21 Nov., 235 – 3 Jan., 236; Greek). His tomb was discovered by de Rossi in 1854, in the catacomb of St Calixtus, as well as those of SS Fabian, Lucius, and Eutychian (Papal crypt).

St Fabian (236 – 250; Roman) divided the City into seven deaconries, organized the administration of the catacombs, and the distribution of alms to the poor. He was martyred under Decius, 20 Jan., 250.

St Cornelius (April, 251 – June, 253; Roman) opposed the schism of the rigorist Novatian.

[Novatian, 251.]

St Lucius I (25 June, 253 – 5 March, 254; Roman) continued to show the same leniency as his predecessor and St Cyprian had shown towards those who had sacrificed to idols but had repented, a leniency contrasted with the severity of Novatian.

St Stephen I (254 – 2 Aug., 257; Roman) opposed with vigour the error of those who would rebaptize converted heretics, and upheld the Roman doctrine on that point against St Cyprian and the bishops of Asia Minor.

St Sixtus II (otherwise Xystus) (31 Aug., 257 – 6 Aug., 258; Greek) was reconciled to St Cyprian. St Sixtus was martyred with his deacons, Felicissimus and Agapitus, some days before the deacon St Lawrence.

St Dionysius (22 July, 259 – 26 Dec., 268) condemned Sabellianism, a heresy about the Blessed Trinity.

St Felix I (269 – 274; Roman) approved of the condemnation of Paul of Samosata, pronounced by the synod of Antioch.

St Eutychian (275 – 283).

St Caius (17 Dec., 283 – 22 April, 296; Dalmatian).

St Marcellinus (30 June, 296 – 26 April, or 25 Oct., 304; Roman).

St Marcellus I (308 – 16 Jan., 309; Roman) elected after the longest vacancy in the history of the Popes; reorganized the see, rebuilding the churches destroyed in the persecution.

St Eusebius (18 April – 17 Aug., 310; Greek).

St Melchiades (2 July, 311 – 11 Jan., 314; African) saw the victory of Constantine over Maxentius, and the 'Edict of Milan', giving liberty to the Church. He held a synod in Rome against the Donatists (schismatics who afterwards became heretics). He was the last Pope buried in the Catacombs.

St Sylvester I (31 Jan., 314 – 31 Dec., 335; Roman). The Pope of " the Peace of the Church ". He erected the basilicas of St Peter (Vatican) and St John (Lateran). He delegated two Roman priests to represent him at the Council of Nicæa.

St Mark (18 Jan. – 7 Oct., 336; Roman) built two basilicas in Rome—St Mark and St Balbina.

St Julius I (6 Feb., 337 – 12 April, 352; Roman). He defended St Athanasius against the Arians and semi-Arians, held a synod in Rome against Arianism (340 – 41), arranged the meeting of the Council of Sardica (Sofia) (342), and erected in Rome the basilica of the Twelve apostles (Basilica Juliana).

Liberius (17 May, 352 – 24 Sept., 366; Roman) was treated with great harshness by the emperor Constantius for his refusal to condemn St Athanasius and underwent a long exile in Berea, during which the emperor set up an anti-pope. Liberius has been severely judged for signing a statement of faith that could be given a heretical meaning. He founded the Basilica of St Mary Major.
[Felix II, 355.]

St Damasus I (Oct., 366 – 11 Dec., 384; Spaniard) condemned the Apollinarists (heresy on the Incarnation), Macedonians (heresy on the Holy Ghost) (synods 368, 369), fixed the Canon of Scripture (374), and charged his learned secretary, St Jerome, to revise the translation of the Bible. He opened up the Catacombs and composed many inscriptions for the tombs of the martyrs.
[Ursicinus, 366.]

St Siricius (17 Dec., 384 – 26 Nov., 399; Roman) acted vigorously as the chief pastor of the Church and was the first to be called ' Pope '. He and his predecessor began the steady resistance to domination by the emperors at Constantinople. He is the author of a famous declaration of the Primacy of the Pope over the whole Church, contained in a letter of 10 Feb., 385, to Himerius of Tarragona. Through the Roman synod of 386 he forbade any episcopal consecration without the consent of the Holy See. He condemned Jovian in the synod of 392 (heresy on morals).

St Anastasius I (399 – 401; Roman).

St Innocent I (401 – 12 March, 417; Roman) continued the ecclesiastical and liturgical organization begun by St Siricius (celibacy of clergy, administration of sacraments, jurisdiction of provincial synods and grouped the Churches of Gaul, Spain and Africa firmly under Rome. His best-known decrees were those to St Victricius of Rouen, Exuperius of Toulouse, and to the Bishop of Gubbio.

St Zozimus (18 March, 417 – 26 Dec., 418; Greek) condemned the Pelagians who had first deceived him, and published his *Epistola tractoria* against them.

St Boniface (28 Dec., 418 – 4 Sept., 422; Roman) obtained the withdrawal of an edict of Theodosius II, which placed Illyria under the authority of the Patriarch of Constantinople. The Balkans began to be an apple of discord between the Holy See and Constantinople—one of the causes which led to the Schism.
[Eulalius, 418.]

St Celestine I (10 Sept., 422 – 27 July, 432; Roman). In 429 he sent St Germanus of Auxerre to Britain to oppose Pelagianism. He also sent St Palladius (431) and St Patrick (432) to evangelize Ireland. St Celestine opposed Nestorianism (heresy on the Incarnation) in a Roman synod (430) and sent three legates to represent him at the Council of Ephesus (431). He addressed to the Bishops of Gaul a letter refuting semi-Pelagianism. He founded the Basilica of St Sabina on the Aventine.

St Sixtus III (31 July, 432 – 28 March, 440; Roman) was a great builder. He restored and richly decorated St Mary Major, and St Laurence-outside-the-Walls. He opposed Nestorius and the Pelagian, Julian of Eclanum, and had to maintain his rights over Illyria against Proclus, Patriarch of Constantinople.

St Leo I, the Great (29 Sept., 440 – 10 Nov., 461; Roman) was one of the most famous Popes of history and one of the most illustrious defenders of the

Faith. He is regarded as one of the 'Fathers of the Church'. He opposed the Pelagians and Manichæans in Italy, the Priscillianists in Spain, and the Monophysites in the East. He dominated the Council of Chalcedon (451) and rejected the 28th article of that Council which gave second rank in the Church to the Patriarch of Constantinople. He also maintained his rights in Illyria, established a permanent legate at the court of Constantinople and greatly strengthened the whole administrative system of the Western Church. He is also famous for his courageous attitude at the time of the invasions of Attila and Genseric.

St Hilary (461 – 28 Feb., 468; Sardinian) exercised his authority vigorously with regard to ecclesiastical discipline in Southern Gaul and Spain.

St Simplicius (468 – 10 March, 483; Roman) interposed to put down the Monophysites in Alexandria, and resisted the attempt of the Patriarch of Constantinople to claim second rank in the Church.

St Felix III (483 – 492; Roman) energetically opposed the Monophysites, denounced the *Henoticon* (a decree of union with heretics) inspired by Acacius, Patriarch of Constantinople, whom he excommunicated. This occasioned a schism for 35 years. St Felix encouraged the faithful in Africa, who were presecuted by Gunthamond, King of the Vandals.

St Gelasius I (1 March, 492 – 21 Nov., 496; Roman). A great Pope, he upheld the authority of the Holy See against Acacius, was on good terms with Theodoric the Great, King of the Ostrogoths, opposed the Manichæans and the Pelagians, and put an end to the pagan festival of the Lupercalia.

Anastasius II (496 – 498; Roman) congratulated Clovis on his conversion, opposed the schism of Acacius, and condemned Traducianism (heresy on creation).

St Symmachus (22 Nov., 498 – 19 July, 514; Sardinian). Inserted the *Gloria* in the Mass on Sundays.

[Laurence, 498.]

St Hormisdas (20 July, 514 – 6 Aug., 523; Roman). The schism of Acacius (484 – 519) came to an end, the bishops of the East adopting the Confession of Faith, called the *Formula of Hormisdas*, in which the Primacy of the Roman See is strongly set forth.

St John I (13 Aug., 523 – 18 May, 526; Tuscan). Sent by Theodoric, Gothic King of Italy, to Constantinople, he crowned the Emperor Justin I. On his return he was thrown into prison by Theodoric (an Arian) in reprisal for measures against the Arians by Justin I. There he died. He is honoured as a martyr.

St Felix IV (526 – 530; Samnite), being consulted by St Cæsarius of Arles on the subject of semi-Pelagianism, sent a doctrinal letter, which was proclaimed as the law of the Church at the Council of Orange (529). Felix IV nominated Boniface II as his successor.

Boniface II (17 Sept., 530 – Oct., 532; Ostrogoth) confirmed the decrees of the Council of Orange, thus giving them universal authority. He again maintained the rights of the Holy See over Illyria.

[Dioscorus, 530.]

John II (2 Nov., 532 – 8 May, 535; Roman). He was Mercurius, priest of the parish of St Clement, and the first to change his name on becoming Pope, a custom which has since become general.

St Agapitus I (535 – 22 April, 536; Roman).

St Silverius (536 – 537; Roman). After the taking of Rome by Belisarius he was arrested, owing to the intrigues of the ambitious Vigilius, and died in exile. He is deemed a martyr. Vigilius had taken his place on 29 March, 537.

Vigilius (538 – 7 June, 555; Roman). Having usurped the Papal throne by illegitimate means, Vigilius received universal recognition after the death of Silverius, and thus became lawful Pope. Contrary to the expectation of the Empress Theodora to whom he owed his elevation, he contended for the Catholic Faith with Justinian. He passed eight years at Constantinople at the time of the dispute of the ' Three Chapters ', finally confirmed the decrees of the Council of Constantinople (553) and died at Syracuse on his return.

Pelagius I (555 – 561; Roman). In 555 there began the Schism of Aquileia and Grado which lasted until 700.

John III (17 July, 561 – 13 July, 574; Roman).

Benedict I (2 June, 575 – 30 July, 579; Roman).

Pelagius II (26 Nov., 579 – 7 Feb., 590; Roman) had much to suffer from the Lombards. He protested against the title of ' Universal Patriarch ' being assumed by the Patriarch of Constantinople (John the Faster) and rejoiced in the conversion of the Visigoths of Spain.

St Gregory I—the Great (3 Sept., 590 – 12 March, 604; Roman). One of the greatest popes of history. He was born about 540 of an illustrious family, and was made Prætor of Rome, an office he abandoned to become a Benedictine monk. He gave his palace on the Coelian Hill to be the monastery of St Andrew (it is from this that three of our English Cardinals—Manning, Vaughan and Griffin—received the title " of St Andrew and St Gregory on the Coelian Hill "). He was sent as Papal envoy to Constantinople. Anxious for the conversion of the heathen and especially interested in England, he obtained leave to work there himself, and even set out, but the clamour of the people obliged the Pope to recall him. When he became Pope himself he sent St Augustine and his companions on this mission (597) and planned the organization of the Church in England—two archbishops each with 12 suffragans, and Canterbury to be the Primatial See.

St Gregory reformed the ecclesiastical chant—hence called Gregorian —modified the Canon of the Mass and put the *Pater Noster* in its present position, regulated the ' Stations ' (as shown in the Missal) and left numerous writings on Christian life and doctrine; he did much to develop Christian spirituality and monasticism. Owing to the neglect of Rome by the Greek emperors, St Gregory was obliged to take upon himself much of the civil government of Rome. In protest against the growing ambition of the Patriarchs of Constantinople who called themselves ' The Œcumenical Patriarch ' he took the title " Servants of the servants of God ", which is still used by the Pope today.

St Sabinian (13 Sept., 604 – 22 June, 606; Tuscan).

Boniface III (19 Feb. – 12 Nov., 607; Roman).

St Boniface IV (15 Sept., 608 – 25 May, 615; Italian). He arranged with Mellitus, Bishop of London, certain questions concerning points of discipline in which the British practice differed from the actual usage of Rome.

St Deusdedit or Adeodatus I (19 Oct., 615 – 8 Nov., 618; Roman) was the first to use ' *Papal Bulls* '.

Boniface V (23 Dec., 619 – 25 Oct., 625; Italian) continued the organization of the Church in England, and in 625 granted Primatial rights to the see of Canterbury according to the design of St Gregory the Great.

Honorius I (3 Nov., 625 – 12 Oct., 638; Italian). A fervent lover of religious art. He failed to grasp the meaning of the theory of the Patriarch Sergius of Constantinople concerning the two wills in Christ; this had the effect of encouraging the Monothelite heresy, and for this he was afterwards condemned by the Sixth General Council (680). He prescribed that when either of the English metropolitans died, his successor should be consecrated by the other, so as to save the long journey to Rome.

Severinus (elected 2 Oct., 638, consecrated 28 May, 640 – 2 Aug., 640; Roman). Condemned the *Ecthesis* (a decree by the Greek emperor Heraclius in favour of the Monothelites.

John IV (24 Dec., 640 – 12 Oct., 642; Dalmatian). Condemned the Monothelite heresy in a Roman synod (640), and explained the error of Honorius.

Theodore I (24 Nov., 642 – 13 May, 649; Greek) energetically opposed the Monothelite heresy, which was upheld by the Patriarchs Pyrrhus and Paul of Constantinople.

St Martin I (July, 649 – 16 Sept., 655; Italian). By his condemnation of the Monothelites at the Lateran Council (Oct., 649) he drew on himself the hatred of Constans II and was, by order of this emperor, arrested in the Lateran Palace (653) and taken to Constantinople. He was condemned to death, treated with cruelty, and banished to the Chersonese, where he died. He is honoured as a martyr.

St Eugene I (10 Aug., 654 – 2 June, 657; Roman). He was elected during the life-time of St Martin. He tried to reconcile the emperor with the Church, but without sacrificing orthodoxy.

St Vitalian (30 July, 657 – 27 Jan., 672; Italian) sent a learned Greek monk, Theodore of Tarsus, to be Archbishop of Canterbury, with full jurisdiction over all the Church of the Angles.

Adeodatus II (11 April, 672 – 17 June, 676; Roman) opposed the Monothelites.

Donus (2 Nov., 676 – 11 April, 678; Roman) obliged the Archbishop of Ravenna to acknowledge the authority of the Holy See.

St Agatho (27 June, 678 – 10 Jan., 681; a Greek of Sicily) condemned the Monothelites in a synod at Rome (680) and, with the emperor, called the Sixth General Council, sending to it the Definition of Faith on the Monothelite heresy. He reduced the number of English sees to twelve, with one metropolitan.

St Leo II (elected Dec., 681, consecrated 17 Aug., 682 – 3 July, 683; Sicilian). He confirmed the decrees of the Sixth General Council, had them translated into Latin and sent them to the bishops of Spain; put an end to the schism of Ravenna.

St Benedict II (elected 683, consecrated July, 684 – 8 May, 685; Roman). He endeavoured to make all the West receive the decrees of the Sixth General Council.

John V (23 July, 685 – 2 Aug., 686; Syrian).

Conon (Oct., 686 – 22 Sept., 687; Greek).

[Theodore, 687.]

[Paschal, 687.]

8

St Sergius I (15 Dec., 687–Sept., 701; of Syrian origin, born in Sicily) refused to confirm the decisions of the Council 'in Trullo' (a council at Constantinople, composed almost entirely of Eastern bishops, whose decrees on discipline were animated by a spirit of hostility to Rome) (692).

He consecrated St Willibrord as Archbishop of Frisia and introduced the custom of singing the *Agnus Dei* at Mass.

John VI (30 Oct., 701 – 11 Jan., 705; Greek). He—like two of his predecessors—did justice to St Wilfrid when driven from his see by the kings of Mercia and Northumbria.

John VII (1 March, 705 – 18 Oct., 707; Greek) refused to confirm the decrees of the Council ' in Trullo '.

Sisinnius (18 Jan. – 4 Feb., 708; Syrian).

Constantine I (25 March, 708 – 9 April, 715; Syrian) received the submission of the Archbishop of Ravenna. He made the journey to Nicomedia, at the command of the emperor Justinian II, who desired his confirmation of the Council ' in Trullo '. The Pope, however, refused to confirm it.

St Gregory II (19 May, 715 – 11 Feb., 731; Roman) prevented the conquest of Rome by the Lombards, and opposed the emperor Leo III, the Isaurian, who wished to abolish the use of images; a Roman synod condemned the Iconoclast heresy (729). This Pope consecrated St Boniface, an English monk, and sent him as bishop to be the apostle of Germany.

St Gregory III (18 March, 731 – 10 Dec, 741; Syrian) broke off relations with the Court of Constantinople on account of the heresy of the emperor. Threatened by the Lombards, he appealed for aid to the Franks, but Charles Martel refused it. This Pope made St Boniface archbishop of the whole of Germany, and reformed the Church in Gaul. In 735 he sent the pallium to Egbert of York and thus constituted a second archbishopric for the north of England. He greatly encouraged the Roman painters.

St Zachary (3 Dec., 741 – 23 March, 752; Greek) tried to arrest the progress of the Lombards, and obtained a truce for 20 years (742). The most notable feature of this reign is the Pope's steady support of St Boniface, who in his name crowned Pepin King of the Franks.

Stephen II (III) (26 March, 752 – 26 April, 757; Roman). He concluded a truce for 40 years with Aistulf, king of the Lombards, but as it was not faithfully kept he crossed the Alps—the first Pope to do so—and went to ask the intervention of Pepin, whom he crowned with his sons in St Denis (754). Pepin invaded Italy, defeated Aistulf, and, despite the protests of the emperor, made over a great part of the conquered territory to the Pope. This is the origin of the Papal States and the great turning-point in Papal history.

St Paul I (29 May, 757 – 28 June, 767; Roman), brother of Stephen III, whose policy of alliance with the Franks he continued, in order to hold in check Desiderius, king of the Lombards. Political relations with Constantinople now definitely broken off. He took under his protection the monks expelled from Constantinople by the Iconoclasts. The spurious ' Donation of Constantine ' was most probably drawn up at this time.

[Constantine, 767.]

[Philip, 768].

Stephen III (IV) (elected 1 Aug., consecrated 7 Aug., 768 – 24 Jan., 772; Sicilian). This Pope was elected after a year of terrible strife and war, caused by the nobles' imposition of a layman as Pope. Whereupon the right of electing Popes was taken from the laity in 769, and restricted to the clergy of Rome. The term cardinal' now first appears in the records. The just use of images was proclaimed orthodox.

Adrian I (1 Feb., 772 – 26 Dec., 795; Roman) was aided by Charlemagne against the Lombard king, whose kingdom was suppressed in 774, whereupon the Exarchate and the Pentapolis became definitely States of the Church. Charlemagne confirmed the ' Donation of Pepin ', but refused to receive the decision of the Second General Council of Nicæa (787) about the veneration of images. In 787 the Pope sent two legates to visit England, and he approved a third metropolitan see at Lichfield at the request of Offa, King of Mercia. An indefatigable restorer of churches.

St Leo III (27 Dec., 795 – 12 June, 816; Roman). A revolt of the Romans obliged him to seek refuge at Paderborn. Charlemagne came in person to Rome to investigate the accusations made against him. On Christmas Day, 800, St Leo III crowned him Emperor of the Romans. Latin Christianity and a Teutonic Kingship called the Holy Roman Empire were thus equated as the two ruling powers of the West. He reversed the decision of Adrian I and abolished the archbishopric at Lichfield, 803.

Stephen IV (V) (elected 12, consecrated 22 June, 816 – 24 Jan., 817; Roman). This Pope and the next were elected by the Roman clergy only.

St Paschal I (25 Jan., 817 – 11 Feb., 824; Roman).

Eugenius II (6 June, 824 – 27 Aug., 827; Roman). In concert with the emperor, this Pope promulgated the " Constitution of Lothair " (Lothair I, Holy Roman Emperor), Nov. 824, which gave back to the laity their share in the election of the Popes and made the emperor the judge of the validity of the election.

Valentine (Aug. – Oct., 827; Roman).

Gregory IV (end of 827 – Jan., 844; Roman) named St Anschar his legate for the Scandinavian missions. He introduced the Feast of All Saints into the Roman calendar.

[John.]

Sergius II (844 – 27 Jan., 847; Roman) was a weak and venal ruler. In 846 the Saracens entered Rome and sacked the tombs of the Apostles.

St Leo IV (elected Jan., consecrated 10 April, 847 – 17 July, 855; Roman), " the last of the Old Roman Popes " (Fortescue); from him derives the term ' Leonine City ' on account of the wall built by him round the Vatican quarter. He respected the rights of the empire, whilst maintaining those of the Holy See, especially in regard to Papal elections. He blessed and gave confirmation to Alfred, son of Ethelwulf—later King Alfred the Great.

Benedict III (29 Sept., 855 – 7 April, 858; Roman). (It is here that the fable—of Eastern origin perhaps— about ' Pope Joan ' is placed. She is supposed to have reigned from 855 to 858).

[Anastasius, 855.]

St Nicholas the Great (24 April, 858 – 13 Nov., 867; Roman). He enforced the submission of the Archbishop of Ravenna, annulled the election of Photius to the see of Constantinople, and welcomed the Bulgarians to the Latin rite. The first Pope to be solemnly crowned.

Adrian II (14 Dec., 867 – 14 Dec., 872; Roman) upheld Hincmar, Bishop of Laon, against Hincmar, Archbishop of Rheims and Charles the Bald, King of the Franks. He condemned Photius (Eighth General Council, 869) but the Bulgarians fell back into the obedience of Constantinople. Moravia, however, converted by St Cyril and St Methodius, remained Latin.

John VIII (14 Dec., 872 – 16 Dec., 882; Roman) crowned Charles the Bald emperor (Christmas, 875). Being exiled from Rome by a party faction, he went to France and there crowned Louis the Stammerer king. He also crowned the emperor Charles the Fat (881) but received no help from him against the Saracens. He encouraged the apostolate of St Cyril and St Methodius, and approved of the Slav liturgy. During this reign, Photius obtained a new council (879), which rehabilitated him, and which John VIII confirmed. He was the first Pope to be assassinated.

Marinus I (Dec., 882 – May, 884; Tuscan). This is the first instance of a bishop being elected Pope (he was Bishop of Cervetri). He favoured the *Schola Anglorum*, the headquarters of the English in Rome. This Pope was also called Martin II, and his later namesake Martin III.

St Adrian III (17 May, 884 – Sept., 885; Roman).

Stephen V (VI) (885 – 14 Sept., 891; Roman). He put the emperor Basil the Macedonian on his guard against Photius. In a letter to Swatopluk, Duke of Moravia, he forbade the use of the Slavonic liturgy, which had been sanctioned by John VIII.

Formosus (6 Oct., 891 – 4 April, 896; Italian) was Bishop of Porto. He had been deposed and excommunicated by John VIII (30 June, 876) but freed from ecclesiastical censure by Marinus (Martin II, 883). The Dark Age of the Papacy now begins and lasts until Leo IX (1049).

Boniface VI (April, 896; Roman), reigned for 15 days.

Stephen VI (VII) (May, 896 – Aug., 897; Roman). He held a trial of his predecessor's corpse for having left his see of Porto for that of Rome, and annulled his ordinations. However, a rising took place, and Stephen was strangled in prison.

Romanus (Aug. – Nov., 897).

Theodore II (Dec., 897; Roman). In a reign of 20 days he rehabilitated Formosus, and regularized the ordinations made by him, which Stephen VII had annulled. It is probable that he perished by a violent death.

John IX (Jan., 898 – Jan., 900; Roman). He confirmed the rehabilitation of Formosus, and decreed that henceforth the Papal elections should take place in the presence of a delegate of the emperor.

Benedict IV (May or June, 900 – July, 903; Roman). This Pope was a reformer. The Church passed now through a terrible century, in which intrigues, factions and the violence of local tyrants determined Papal elections and subjected the Papacy to a degrading and vexatious dependence.

Leo V (July – Sept., 903; Roman). Deposed and murdered.
[Christopher (autumn 903 – Jan., 904) dethroned Leo V, and was himself dethroned and murdered by Sergius III.]

Sergius III (29 Jan., 904 – 14 April, 911; Roman) owed his elevation to the powerful family of Theophylact, his wife Theodora the Elder, and their two daughters, Theodora the Younger and Marozia.

11

Anastasius III (April, 911 – June, 913; Roman).

Lando (Aug., 913 – March, 914; Lombard).

John X (March, 914 – May, 928; Italian). Owed his elevation to the Papacy to the influence of Theodora. He struggled, however, energetically against the Saracens. Overthrown and murdered by Marozia.

Leo VI (5 May, 928 – Dec., 928); Roman). Rome was dominated during this Pontificate by Marozia, who appointed this Pope and his two successors.

Stephen VII (VIII) (929 – Feb., 931; Roman).

John XI (March, 931 – Dec., 935); son of Marozia.

Leo VII (9 Jan., 936 – July, 939; Roman). Appointed Pope, like his three successors, by Marozia's son, Alberic II. Reformed the monasteries with the help of St Odo, Abbot of Cluny.

Stephen VIII (IX) (14 July, 939 – Oct., 942; Roman).

Marinus II (Oct., 942 – May, 946; Roman), otherwise Martin III. He was zealous for the Cluniac Reform. This was a troubled time for the whole of Italy—feudal wars and incursions of the Saracens.

Agapitus II (May, 946 – Dec., 955; Roman). Conferred large powers on the Archbishops of Hamburg.

John XII (16 Dec., 955 – 14 May, 964; Roman). He was Octavian, son of Alberic II, and was made Pope at 16 by the influence of his family. He is one of the few Popes of scandalous morals. He crowned Otto I as emperor at Rome (962). The emperor later deposed John XII and drove him from his throne. He regained it, but was murdered.

(There has always been a doubt whether John XII or Leo VIII (Dec., 963) was the lawful Pope of the time. Often deemed an anti-pope, Leo VIII is treated as lawful by the *Annuario Pontificio*).

Benedict V (964 – 965; Roman). Deposed by Emperor Otto I in June, 964, who thereupon restored Leo VIII (see above).

John XIII (1 Oct., 965 – 6 Sept., 972; Roman). He relied on the support of Otto I, who protected him against the revolts of the Romans. He crowned Otto II, 25 Dec., 967.

Benedict VI (19 Jan., 973 – July, 974; Roman): deposed and murdered by factious nobles.

(Between Benedict VI and Benedict VII some lists have put in a Donus II, who never existed. It is simply a copyist's mistake.)

[Boniface VII, 974.]

Benedict VII (Oct., 974 – July, 983; Roman): appointed by the emperor. This Pope tried to reform abuses in the Church, especially by laws against simony.

John XIV (10 Dec., 983 – 20 Aug., 984): Pietro Campanora, who had been Bishop of Pavia. Anxious to make the needed reforms in the Church. He was imprisoned in the Castle of St Angelo and died there, probably murdered by the anti-pope Boniface VII.

John XV (Aug., 985 – March, 996; Roman) was a learned Pope, and a friend of the Cluniac monks, but too much attached to the interests of his relations. He was the first Pope to perform a canonization properly so-called, that of St Ulrich (993).

(The old lists counted two Popes between John XIV and John XV, Boniface VII (Franco) who was certainly an anti-pope, and another John XV, supposed to have been elected but never consecrated. In reality he did not exist. It was this which changed the true order of the Popes named John).

Gregory V (3 May, 996 – 18 Feb., 999): Bruno, son of Duke of Carinthia appointed by the emperor. The first German Pope. He authorized the replacement of secular canons at Canterbury Cathedral by Benedictine monks. He fought energetically against simony, and made Robert, King of France, respect the marriage laws. Poisoned by the Roman nobles.

[John XVI, 997, supported by Crescentius II against Gregory V (997 – 998).]

Sylvester II (2 April, 999 – 12 May, 1003). Gerbert, born in Auvergne, the first French Pope. So fond of science that he was deemed a magician. He tried, in concert with the energetic emperor Otto III, who had appointed him, to organize the Christian world—gave the title of king to St Stephen of Hungary, founded the Archbishopric of Gnesen, in Poland, and that of Gran (Esztergom) in Hungary.

John XVII (13 June – 6 Nov., 1003; Roman). This Pope and his two successors were the nominees of the nobles —all-powerful since the death of Otto III (1003).

John XVIII (25 Dec., 1003 – July, 1009; Phasinus Roman).

Sergius IV Pietro Buccaporca (31 July, 1009 – 12 May, 1012; Roman).

[An anti-pope called " Gregory VI ".]

Benedict VIII (20 April, 1012 – 9 April, 1024), Theophylact II, second son of Gregory, Count of Tusculum, raised to the Papacy through the influence of his kindred. Crowned St Henry II, emperor, and on this occasion introduced the ' Filioque ' into the Creed.

He ordered the Nicene Creed to be sung in the Mass after the Gospel. He worked for the reform of the Church. He visited St Henry at Bamberg, in 1020, and consecrated the cathedral in that city.

John XIX (May, 1024 – 6 Dec., 1032), Romanus, brother of Benedict VIII, but a bad Pope. He published the first indulgence to which was attached the giving of alms as a condition.

Benedict IX (1032 – 1048), Theophylact III. Raised to the Papal dignity in spite of his extreme youth, by the tyrants of Rome—he was the nephew of the last two Popes. He had three separate terms of office as Pope: (1) 1032 – 44, (2) 1045 (April to May), (3) 1047 – 48. Benedict died about 1049.

Sylvester III (Feb. to April, 1044). His election is of doubtful validity, and his reign ended with the return of Benedict IX.

Gregory VI (5 May, 1045 – 20 Dec., 1046, died 1047; Roman), John Gratian. Benedict IX having offered to relinquish the See for a compensation, Gregory paid the money. His election therefore is of doubtful validity. Gregory was a good, charitable, and popular man, but was deposed, together with Benedict IX and Sylvester III, by the emperor, Henry III, at the Council of Sutri, Dec., 1046. He died at Cologne.

Clement II (24 Dec., 1046 – 9 Oct., 1047; German), Suidger of Saxony, Bishop of Bamberg: appointed by Henry III. He tried to reform abuses in the Church.

Damasus II (17 July – 9 Aug., 1048; German), Poppo, Bishop of Brixen, appointed by Henry III.

St Leo IX (12 Feb., 1049 – 19 April, 1054), Bruno, Count of Dagsbourg, in Alsace, Bishop of Toul from 1027. He was also appointed Pope by Henry III. The first of the 'Apostolic pilgrims', Popes who were obliged, or who chose, to travel in fulfilment of their functions. He undertook journeys of visitation, and presided in person over the Councils of Lateran, Pavia, Rheims, and Mainz, fighting against lay-investitures, simony, clerical marriages, and all ecclesiastical abuses, with the help of Hildebrand, Humbert of Moyenmoutier, and Hugh of Cluny. The schism of the Greek Church was accomplished finally under his reign, though Michael Cerularius alone was actually excommunicated (16 July, 1054).

Victor II (13 April, 1055 – 28 July, 1057), Count Gebhard of Dollenstein, Bishop of Eichstadt. The last Pope to be named by an emperor. He held a great Council of reform at Florence, and sent Hildebrand and other legates to promote reform in France (Councils of Lyons and Toulouse, 1055, 1056).

Stephen IX (X) (2 Aug., 1057 – 29 March, 1058), Frederick, son of Duke Gozelo of Lorraine. He had been one of the legates sent to Constantinople against Michael Cerularius in 1054, and was the first Pope freely elected by the Roman clergy since Paschal I. A great reformer.

[Benedict X, 1058.]

Nicholas II (24 Jan., 1059 – 27 July, 1061), Gerard of Burgundy, Bishop of Florence. He made a decree regulating finally the privilege of the cardinals to be the sole electors of the Pope and abolishing all the emperor's rights in the matter. By this measure the Papacy achieved freedom. He also recognized the Norman, Robert Guiscard, as Prince of Apulia, Calabria and Sicily.

Alexander II (1 Oct., 1061 – 21 April, 1073), Anselm of Baggio, near Milan,

Bishop of Lucca, The first of the " Gregorian " or " Hildebrandine " school. A tried and experienced reformer, he continued to fight the three great evils of the time, lay-investitures, simony, and clerical concubinage. He was greatly helped, too, by St Peter Damian. At the end of the Saxon period in England the four principal sees were held uncanonically, and the clergy as a rule were lax and ignorant. The Pope, therefore, encouraged William the Conqueror in his project of claiming the English throne. His legates crowned William and deposed Stigand, who had recognized the anti-pope Benedict X, and usurped the see of Canterbury to which see the Pope nominated Lanfranc of Pavia, formerly Prior of Bec, and then Abbot of Caen.

(Honorius II, 1061.)

St Gregory VII (22 April, 1073 – 25 May, 1085): Hildebrand. One of the greatest Popes of history, his pontificate was a turning-point in European civilization. Born at Soana, in Tuscany, about 1020, he was associated with the Popes in all the affairs of the Church from the time of Leo IX. He was under Cluniac influence, the most potent force for reform in the Middle Ages. He aimed especially at the abolition of lay-investiture as the source of the other abuses in the Church, and here he came into violent conflict with the emperor, Henry IV. He excommunicated and deposed the latter and freed his subjects from their allegiance. Henry made his submission at Canossa (Jan. 28, 1077), but soon relapsed. This was the first effective exercise of the celebrated ' Deposing Power'. St Gregory then approved of the choice of Rudolf of Suabia as king of Germany, whereupon Henry took Rome, and the Pope was only delivered by the

Normans, under Robert Guiscard. He died in exile at Salerno. He has been much criticized by those who uphold the supremacy of the State over the Church. In England, William the Conqueror introduced the Norman 'Customs', aimed at subjecting the papal authority to the royal in ecclesiastical affairs. By an act dated 1077 the Countess Matilda of Tuscany, the Pope's great ally against the emperor, purported to leave her vast possessions to the Holy See. A part of this territory came into possession early in the following century.

[Clement III, 1084.]

Blessed Victor III (elected 24 May, 1086, consecrated 9 May, 1087 – 16 Sept., 1087), Cardinal Desiderius, Abbot of Monte Cassino. He continued the struggle of Gregory VII against lay-investitures, and died at Monte Cassino.

Blessed Urban II O.S.B. (12 March, 1088 – 29 July, 1099), Odo of Largery, born at Châtillon on the Marne (1042), Cardinal Bishop of Ostia (1078) the second French Pope. He continued the fight against investitures, and against Henry's anti-pope, Clement III (Guibert of Ravenna). He held many local councils for reforming abuses— Melfi (1089), Piacenza (1095), Clermont (1095), where he launched the first Crusade, and Bari (1098), at which St Anselm of Canterbury was present. He had come to lay before the Sovereign Pontiff the wrongs he suffered at the hands of William Rufus, who had forbidden him to go to Rome, and ordered him to renounce obedience to the Pope, except as allowed by the king. Urban II, at the Council of Rome (1099), forbade any cleric henceforth to become the vassal of a layman for ecclesiastical preferment.

Paschal II, a Cluniac, (1099 – 21 Jan., 1118), Rainieri of Bieda, near Viterbo.

Held Councils at Rome (1102), Guastalla (1106), Troyes (1107), Lateran (1107), Benevento (1109). In 1111 he signed a treaty with the emperor, Henry V, in which he yielded the question of investitures, and offered to surrender all the church properties and temporal jurisdictions. This aroused opposition; the struggle was resumed, at the Lateran Council (1112), and Paschal was driven from Rome by Henry V. He confirmed the treaty called 'Truce of God', at the Council of Troja (1115), and refused to allow Henry I of England any exemption from the general law on investitures made by Urban II. Henry I submitted.

[Theodoric, 1100.]

[Albert, 1102.]

[Sylvester IV, 1105.]

Gelasius II O.S.B. (24 Jan., 1118 – 18 Jan., 1119), Giovanni Gaetani, died and was buried at Cluny.

[Gregory VIII, 1118.]

Calixtus II (elected at Cluny 2, crowned 9 Feb., 1119 – 13 Dec., 1124), Guy of Burgundy, Archbishop of Vienne (France). A courageous opponent of lay-investiture, he settled the long contest by the Concordat of Worms (1122) which was confirmed at the First General Council of the Lateran (1123). He had much trouble with Henry I of England, who had again begun to usurp the rights of the Holy See as to appointing and translating bishops, and refused for seven years to recognize the Archbishop of York (Thurstan) consecrated by Calixtus.

Honorius II (15 Dec., 1124 – 14 Feb., 1130), Lambert Scannabecchi, of Fagnano, near Imola. He re-established relations with England, which had been strained almost to breaking by the arbitrary acts of the first three Norman kings.

[Celestine II, 1124.]

1139 ellibacitz introduced

Innocent II (14 Feb., 1130 – 24 Sept., 1143), Gregory Papareschi, was driven to France by the party of the anti-pope Pierleone (Anacletus II). St Bernard and St Norbert supported Innocent, and the end of the schism was celebrated at the Second General Council of the Lateran (1139). In 1138, Archbishop Theobald of Canterbury received from the Pope the title of Legatus Natus, which remained with his successors till the Reformation.

[Anacletus II, 1130.]
[Victor IV, 1138.]

Celestine II (26 Sept., 1143 – 8 March, 1144), Guido di Castello, a Tuscan. The first English cardinal, Robert Pullen, was created by him.

Lucius II (12 March, 1144 – 15 Feb., 1145), Gerard Caccianemici, of Bologna, a Canon Regular, encouraged the religious orders, especially the Premonstratensians: killed while besieging the Capitol.

Blessed Eugenius III (15 Feb., 1145 – 8 July, 1153), Bernard Paganelli of Pisa, a Cistercian, influenced and virtually directed by St Bernard. Theobald of Canterbury attended the Council of Rheims (1148) contrary to the orders of King Stephen, for which he was banished. The Pope, in consequence, laid England for a short time under an interdict. Owing to the disturbances created in Rome by Arnold of Brescia, this Pope had to go twice into exile. He died at Tivoli.

Anastasius IV (12 July, 1153 – 3 Dec., 1154). Conrad of Rome.

Adrian IV (4 Dec., 1154 – 1 Sept., 1159), Nicholas Breakspeare, the only English Pope. He studied in France, and became an Abbot of Canons Regular. Eugenius III created him Cardinal Bishop of Albano, and sent him as Legate to Denmark, Sweden, and Norway. His mission was the beginning of a new age in Scandinavian Catholicism, and on the death of Anastasius IV he was elected Pope. By the Bull *Laudabiliter*, 1155, he handed over the sovereignty of Ireland to Henry II of England. In this reign began the second phase of the long struggle between the Empire and the Papacy. Frederick I (Barbarossa) continually endeavoured to subject the Church to the State. The Popes were driven to ally themselves with the Lombard League of cities against him.

Alexander III (7 Sept., 1159 – 30 Aug., 1181), Rolando Bandinelli of Siena. First of the line of canonist Popes. Under Gratian he taught Canon Law at Bologna, very probably to Thomas Becket. He sustained a long and heroic struggle against the Emperor Frederick I from whom he had to take refuge in France (and the anti-popes named by him), and more than once excommunicated him. This, together with the crushing defeat of Legnano, brought Frederick to make a full submission at Venice (1177). Henry II of England for six years 1164–1170 persecuted St Thomas Becket, whom Alexander had supported, and whom he canonized 21 Feb., 1173. At the Third General Council of the Lateran (1179), Alexander condemned the Albigenses and Waldenses, and reformed the method of Papal elections, making two-thirds of the cardinals' votes the majority needed for a valid election.

(Anti-popes set up by Barbarossa.)
[Victor IV, 1159 – 1164.]
[Paschal III, 1164.]
[Calixtus III, 1168.]
[Innocent III, 1179 – 1180.]

Lucius III (1 Sept., 1181 – 25 Nov., 1185), Ubaldo Allucingoli of Lucca, a Cistercian, called the Council of Verona (1184), where the Third Crusade was proposed, and also the measures to be taken against heretics (Inquisition).

Urban III (25 Nov., 1185 – 20 Oct., 1187). Uberto Crivelli of Milan. Elected at Verona: died at Ferrara. He had been one of the legates sent by Alexander III to investigate the murder of Becket.

Gregory VIII (21 Oct. – 17 Dec., 1187). Alberto di Morra of Benevento.

Clement III (19 Dec., 1187 – 20 March, 1191), Paul Scholari, Bishop of Palestrina. A great organizer and reformer; he brought about the Third Crusade.

Celestine III (30 March, 1191 – 8 Jan., 1198). Giacinto Buboni.

Innocent III (8 Jan., 1198 – 16 July, 1216), Lothaire dei Conti di Segni, nephew of Clement III, born at Anagni, and became Pope at 37. A man of commanding genius and extraordinary force of character. Perhaps the greatest of all the Popes; the first to call himself ' The Vicar of Christ '. His pontificate was the summit of papal power. His work was greatly hindered by the subversion of the Fourth Crusade (1202 – 4) into a Latin conquest of Constantinople. In the contested Imperial election he claimed the right to arbitrate and his decision was accepted. He arbitated also in the affairs of Spain, Portugal, Poland, Hungary and Bohemia, and in the crisis of the Albigensian heresy saved medieval civilization (1208 – 9). The rise of the Dominican and Franciscan friars and the beginning of the Inquisition date from this time. The Pope set aside the candidates for the see of Canterbury 1207 and nominated Stephen Langton whom he consecrated and created a cardinal. John,

however, refused to allow Langton into the kingdom and for five years England lay under an interdict until 1213. The Fourth General Council of the Lateran (1215) was the crown of a vast edifice of organization and reform.

Honorius III (18 July, 1216 – 18 March, 1227), Cencio Savelli. He approved the Franciscan, Dominican, and Carmelite Orders.

Gregory IX (19 March, 1227 – 22 Aug., 1241), Ugolino dei Conti di Segni, nephew of Innocent III, elected at the age of 85; a canonist and practical diplomatist. He twice excommunicated Frederic II, who was attempting to subjugate the Church. Gregory died before the end of the conflict. He canonized St Francis and St Dominic. He was obliged to legislate for the Inquisition as the lay powers could have no competence in a matter essentially theological.

Celestine IV (25 Oct., – 10 Nov., 1241), Goffredo Castiglione, a Cistercian monk.

Innocent IV (25 June, 1243 – 7 Dec., 1254), Sinibaldo Fieschi, Count of Baragna, born at Genoa. After Alexander III, this Pope was the greatest of the ' Canonist ' Popes, and a consummate man of business. His supreme object was ' the peace of the Church ', which in effect meant the destruction of the House of Hohenstaufen. Curious effects of this struggle were the offer of the Sicilian crown to Edmund of Lancaster, son of Henry III of England and the coronation of his brother Richard of Cornwall, as King of the Romans. Innocent left Rome, and held a General Council at Lyons, in which he excommunicated Frederick II (1245). The struggle now became fiercer and continued after the death of Frederick (1250). During the long struggle with Frederick he exploited fully the taxable capacity of the whole Church in order to meet his expenses, and sought to provide for numerous Italian priests in other countries, particularly in England. Robert Grosseteste, Bishop of Lincoln, led the protest against excessive ' provisions ' which were eventually reduced, 1253.

Alexander IV (12 Dec., 1254 – 25 May, 1261), Rainaldo dei Conti di Segni, nephew of Gregory IX. He greatly favoured the Franciscans and canonized St Clare.

Urban IV (29 Aug., 1261 – 2 Oct., 1264), Jacques Pantaléon, born at Troyes. He was unable to enter Rome, and lived first at Viterbo, and then at Orvieto. He offered the crown of Naples to Louis IX of France who accepted it for his brother, Charles of Anjou, a step which had many and important consequences. He named fourteen cardinals of whom seven were French and instituted the Feast of Corpus Christi (1264).

Clement IV (5 Feb., 1265 – 29 Nov., 1268), Gui Faucoi le Gros of St Gilles-sur-Rhône, Counsellor of St Louis, and Archbishop of Narbonne. During this pontificate both Manfred and Conradin were destroyed. He greatly extended the administration of the Inquisition. After his death there was an interregnum of nearly three years. The conclave at Viterbo lasted so long that the people ended it by lifting the roof off the building.

Blessed Gregory X (1 Sept., 1271 – 10 Jan., 1276), Theobaldo Visconti of Piacenza. He confirmed the Imperial crown to Rudolf of Hapsburg, and called the Second General Council of Lyons at which the re-union of the Greeks with the Church was effected, and the practice of conclaves was regulated by the Constitution *Ubi Periculum*, 1274. He obtained from Philip III of France the *Contat Venaissin* which belonged to the Holy See until 1791.

Blessed Innocent V (20 Jan. to 22 June, 1276), Peter of Tarantaise, born at Champigny, in Savoy. Reputed author of *Ave Verum Corpus*. The first Dominican Pope.

Adrian V (11 July – 18 Aug., 1276). Ottobon dei Fieschi, nephew of Innocent IV. Had been Legate in England to negotiate between Henry III and the barons led by Simon de Montfort.

John XXI (8 Sept., 1276 – 20 May, 1277), Peter Juliani, a Portuguese known as Petrus Hispanus. A celebrated theologian and great student of the natural sciences and of (Arabian) medicine. He had been physician to Gregory X. Accidently killed by collapse of his work-room. He was the author of the *Summulae Logicales*, which served for three centuries as a textbook of logic. (N.B.—There was no John XX.)

Nicholas III (25 Nov., 1277 – 22 Aug., 1280). Giovanni Gaëtano Orsini. He made great efforts to reconcile the rival bodies into which the Franciscan Order was at this time divided. He sent ambassadors to Mongolia and called Kilwardby to Rome as a cardinal, to make way at Canterbury for Peckham, 1278. He practised nepotism widely as recorded by Dante, *Inf*. XIX, 68 – 74.

Martin IV (22 Feb., 1281 – 28 March, 1285), Simon of Brion, in the diocese of Sens. He was the second Pope of that name but called IV because there had been two Popes named Marinus. He greatly favoured the Carmelite and Augustinian Friars. He excommunicated Michael Paleologus, which led to the renewal of the Greek schism, and Peter III of Aragon in an effort to save Sicily for the French.

18

Honorius IV (2 April, 1285 – 3 April, 1287), Giacomo Savelli, a Roman. Established chairs for Oriental languages at the university of Paris.

Nicholas IV (22 Feb., 1288 – 4 April, 1292), Girolamo Moschi of Ascoli, the first Franciscan Pope. In 1291 was made the famous 'Taxatio of Pope Nicholas', a permanent assessment of the value of all English benefices. Edward I took one-tenth for six years. Nicholas IV made Charles Martel King of Hungary, 1289.

St Celestine V (5 July –13 Dec., 1294), Pietro del Morrone, a hermit of saintly life, elected after a vacancy of 27 months in the Apostolic See. He was unfitted to rule, and resigned after a few months. Dante's famous words about ' the great refusal ' (*Inf*. III, 59 – 61) are reinforced by Boniface VIII's allusion to his predecessor (*Inf*. XXVII, 106). He died in ' protective custody ', 19 May, 1296.

Boniface VIII (24 Dec., 1294 – 11 Oct., 1303), Benedetto Gaëtani, born at Anagni. Under his reign the first jubilee took place (1300). By the famous Bull *Clericis Laicis* (1296) he forbade the enforced extra taxation of ecclesiastical property for secular purposes, except for national defence which brought him into conflict with Philip IV of France and Edward I of England. At length the violent quarrel with Philippe le Bel (Philip IV of France) came to a head with the Bull *Unam Sanctam*, 1302, in which Boniface claimed sovereignty over everybody, lay and clerical. Then followed the outrage at Anagni where, as Dante sang (*Purg*. XX, 86 – 88), Christ was again made captive and mocked in the person of His Vicar. Boniface was arrested and maltreated by emissaries and artisans of Philip, and died of shock.

Blessed Benedict XI (22 Oct., 1303 – 7 July, 1304), Nicola Boccasini of Treviso, formerly general of the Dominicans. His problem was to placate Philippe IV without disavowing and condeming Boniface VIII.

Clement V (5 June, 1305 – 20 April, 1314), Bertrand de Got, Archbishop of Bordeaux, elected at Perugia and crowned at Lyons. Detained in France by the critical state of affairs created by the relations of Boniface VIII and Philip the Fair, he established the Papal residence at Avignon, 1309, where it remained for 70 years. In order to avert a ' trial ' of Boniface VIII, he yielded to the pressure of Philip the Fair, and suppressed the Templars, which was one of the French King's objects at the Council of Vienne (1311 – 12). The story of his secret bargain with Philip before election is not true. He created 24 cardinals of whom 22 were French, and canonized Celestine V in 1313.

John XXII (7 Aug., 1316 – 4 Dec., 1334) Jacques Duèse of Cahors. Elected at Lyons, after a vacancy of two years and three months, at the age of 72 he lived at Avignon, of which he had been bishop. He was a remarkable administrator. He vigorously opposed Louis of Bavaria, a candidate for the Empire, in whose pay and service was William of Ockham, a famous English schoolman, and the Fraticelli (Franciscan extremists called ' the Spirituals '); they set up an anti-pope (Pierre of Corbière). John strongly maintained the rights of the Holy See against Louis and all his supporters; and condemned Marsilius of Padua, who had written a revolutionary work, the *Defensor Pacis*, subordinating the Pope to a General Council and the Council to the Emperor.

[' Nicholas V ', 1328.]

Benedict XII (20 Dec., 1334 – 25 April, 1342), Jacques Fournier of Saverdun in Languedoc, a Cistercian. He and the next four Popes were all elected at Avignon. He is said to have been the first to wear the triple crown. He would have returned to Rome but was prevented by the French King. A pious and austere Pope, he reformed the Roman Curia and the Religious Orders. Built the Papal palace at Avignon.

Clement VI (7 May, 1342 – 6 Dec., 1352), Pierre Roger, a Benedictine who became Archbishop of Rouen. Open-handed and artistic, a politician and a diplomat, but fond of luxury and magnificence, he bought the city of Avignon from Queen Joan of Naples in 1348. Here was the germ of the Great Schism, for this act exasperated the Italians, already annoyed at the desertion of Rome, and by the appointment of an enormous majority of French cardinals. He dangerously developed the Papal system of taxing the whole Church. He fixed the jubilee for every 50th year. In England, Edward III, by the statutes of Provisors and Praemunire, checked the appointment of foreigners to English benefices. From 1347 to 1354 Rome was disturbed by the agitator Cola di Rienzi and made almost independent of the Pope.

Innocent VI (18 Dec., 1352 – 12 Sept., 1362), Etienne Aubert of Mont (diocese of Limoges). He brought about the Peace of Bretigny between France and England, 1360. He tried to reform the Roman Curia, protested against the Golden Bull of the Emperor Charles IV (1356) (which abolished the Papal rights in the election of the German emperors) and by the help of the Spanish Cardinal Albornoz, who was the second founder of the Temporal Power, regained the Papal States which had almost entirely fallen under the power of local despots.

Blessed Urban V (elected 28 Sept., consecrated 6 Nov., 1362 – 19 Dec., 1370) Guillaume Grimoard of Grisac, a Benedictine abbot who was not a cardinal when elected. He recalled Albornoz and thereby nearly lost the Papal States through employing French legates. In 1367 he returned to Rome, but was unable to stay there, and died at Avignon.

Gregory XI (30 Dec., 1370 – 27 March, 1378), Pierre Roger of Beaufort, nephew of Clement VI; the last French Pope. His desire to restore the Papacy to Rome and to regain lost authority in Italy was strengthened by St Catherine of Siena and he returned (1377). The 'Babylonian Captivity' had lasted for seventy-three years.

Urban VI (8 April, 1378 – 15 Oct., 1389), Bartolommeo Prignano of Naples, Archbishop of Bari—the last to be elected Pope without having been a cardinal. The election was conducted amid the clamour and threats of a mob demanding a Roman or at least an Italian Pope. It has however been generally deemed valid. Urban from the outset behaved with such harshness and violence that the majority of the cardinals repudiated their allegiance to him, declared the election invalid and on Sept., 20, 1378, elected at Fondi the French cardinal, Robert of Geneva, as 'Clement VII'. This was invalid, and disastrous. It caused 'The Great Schism', which lasted 40 years (1378 – 1417). St Catherine of Siena (d. 1380) who supported Urban laboured greatly but in vain to end the schism which rapidly became political, the Kings and Princes taking sides according to their interests or antipathies. During his reign, Wyclif, almost the sole English medieval heretic, was condemned.

(Anti-Popes at Avignon.)

[Clement VII, 1378 – 1394.]

[Benedict XIII, 1394 – 1417. (Pedro di Luna, a Spaniard). At Avignon till 1408, then at Peniscola, Spain. Died 1423 or 24].

[Clement VIII, 1417 – abd. 1429, but was ignored from the first.]

Boniface IX (2 Nov., 1389 – 1 Oct., 1404), Pietro Tomacelli of Naples. He expressed a desire to end the schism, but gave great scandal by an excessive attention to his revenues. Canonized St John of Bridlington. In 1392 he was driven out of Rome, but returned Dec. 1393.

Innocent VII (17 Oct., 1404 – 6 Nov., 1406), Cosimo dei Migliorati, a Neapolitan. He had undertaken to resign if ' Benedict XIII ' would do likewise and intended to call a Council to end the schism, but died before he could accomplish it.

Gregory XII (30 Nov., 1406 – 4 June, 1415, died 18 Sept., 1417), Angelo Correr, a Venetian, nearly 80 years of age. He had given the same undertaking as Innocent VII but as he persistently delayed his proferred abdication was abandoned by his cardinals, who united with those of Avignon to hold a Council at Pisa (1409). Next, in 1414, the Council of Constance, summoned to Rome by the Pisan Pope, John XXIII, but fixed at Constance by Sigismund, King of the Romans, called upon Gregory and Benedict XIII to appear before it. Gregory decided to abdicate for the peace of the Church. The Council deposed John XXIII and Benedict XIII.

(Anti-Popes elected by Council of Pisa.)

[Alexander V, Peter Philargos (June, 1409 – May, 1410; Greek).]

[John XXIII, Baldassare Cossa, 1410 – 1415. Submitted to deposition by Council of Constance, May, 1415.]

Martin V (11 Nov., 1417 – 20 Feb., 1431), Odo Colonna, a Roman, elected at Constance. He had to contend against the theory that a General Council is superior to the Pope, and to fight against the heresy of Hus. He dissolved the Council of Constance, April 22, 1418, and arranged for a Council at Basle. He restored order, and recovered the States of the Church but did not initiate reform.

Eugene IV (3 March, 1431 – 23 Feb., 1447), Gabriele Condulmier, a Venetian, nephew of Gregory XII. In 1437 he dissolved the Council of Basle and transferred it to Florence, and for the second time effected reunion with the Greeks (1439).

[Felix V (Duke Amadeus of Savoy), 1440. Abdicated 1449. The last anti-pope.]

Nicholas V (6 March, 1447 – 24 March, 1455), Tommaso Parentucelli of Sarzana (Tuscany), succeeded in putting an end to the schism of Basle (1449), celebrated a splendid jubilee (1450), crowned Frederic III in Rome (1452) —the last imperial coronation in Rome. The first of the ' humanist ' Popes, he was a great patron of learning and art, and the founder of the Vatican Library. The old basilica of St Peter was however ruinous and eventually had to be pulled down.

Calixtus III (8 April, 1455 – 6 Aug., 1458), Alonso de Borgia (Borja), born 1378 near Valencia (Spain). During the previous reign the Turks took Constantinople (1453). He was unable to organize a Crusade against them, but they were defeated before Belgrade (1456). Canonized St Osmund of Salisbury and St Vincent Ferrer.

Pius II (19 Aug., 1458 – 15 Aug., 1464). Æneas Sylvius Piccolomini, born near Siena 1405. A patron of the Renaissance. He had been secretary and an adherent of the anti-pope Felix V, but became a loyal servant of the Holy See, and exercised a great influence. He died at Ancona, whilst endeavouring to raise a Crusade against the Turks.

Paul II (30 Aug., 1464 – 26 July, 1471), Pietro Barbo, born 1418 at Venice, fixed the jubilee for every 25th year. Fearing the Renaissance and the humanist imitation of pagan ways of life, he opposed that tendency, and abolished the Court of the Abbreviatori established by his predecessor, Pius II, and the Academy of Pomponius Laetus, thus drawing on himself the hatred of its members and in particular that of Platina, whose *Life of Paul II* was an act of revenge.

Sixtus IV (9 Aug., 1471 – 12 Aug., 1484), Francesco della Rovere of Savona, a Franciscan, born 1414. He employed Perugino, Botticelli, Ghirlandaio and other great painters in the Sistine Chapel, but used undesirable means of raising funds (plurality of benefices, etc.). In this reign, through the Pope's nomination of incompetent and evil-living men to high office, and his promotion of unworthy relatives, the seeds were sown of all the scandals that, for sixty years, made Rome the world's disgrace. In 1478 he issued a Bull sanctioning the Spanish Inquisition set up by Ferdinand of Aragon.

Innocent VIII (29 Aug., 1484 – 25 July, 1492), Giovanni Battista Cibo, born at Genoa. A weak Pope, who tolerated scandals in the Roman court, but endeavoured to end the long feud between the houses of Colonna and Orsini.

Alexander VI (10 Aug., 1492 – 18 Aug., 1503), Roderigo Borgia (Borja), nephew of Calixtus III. He was intelligent, prudent, and politic, but unscrupulous and a man of bad life, utterly unworthy of his high office. He practised the most deplorable nepotism. As Pope he patronized the foreign missions, arts and letters. He also drew a famous line of arbitration between Spain and Portugal in regard to discoveries in the New World. In 1494 Charles VIII of France invaded Italy to take possession of Naples and was welcomed at Florence by Savonarola as a reformer of the Church.

Pius III (22 Sept. – 18 Oct., 1503), Francesco Todeschini, nephew of Pius II. He at once announced his intention of summoning a Council for the much-needed reforms.

Julius II (31 Oct., 1503 – 21 Feb., 1513), Cardinal Giuliano della Rovere, nephew of Sixtus IV. Patron of San Gallo and Michelangelo. Fierce and ambitious, he was too fond of war (League of Cambrai and Holy League). He dreamed of uniting all Italy—delivered from the ' Barbarians '—under the headship of the Papacy. Julius II is regarded as the refounder of the Papal States having recovered and extended them by military action, but he greatly neglected spiritual matters. A great patron of the arts, laid the first stone of St Peter's. Convened the 5th Lateran Council (1512 – 1517).

Leo X (11 March, 1513 – 1 Dec., 1521), Giovanni de' Medici, born at Florence, 1475, made cardinal at 14. A great patron of scholarship and letters (Raphael, Bembo, etc.). Concluded the famous Concordat of Bologna with Francis I (1516), which handed over virtually all preferments in France to the King. He condemned Luther by the Bull *Exsurge Domine*, 1520, and gave to Henry VIII the title ' Defender of the Faith ' for his book against Luther on the Seven Sacraments.

Adrian VI (9 Jan., 1522 – 14 Sept., 1523) Adrian Dedel, born at Utrecht, the last non-Italian Pope until John Paul II. A former tutor of Charles V, he was a zealous and virtuous Pope, who tried to reform the Roman Curia. His austerity made him extremely unpopular in Rome.

Clement VII (18 Nov., 1523 – 25 Sept., 1534), Giulio de' Medici, cousin of Leo X, born 1478, Archbishop of Florence. By his unwise political activities he brought about both the Hapsburg domination of Italy and the Sack of Rome 1527. He saw Germany a prey to religious dissension, the Turks at the walls of Vienna, 1529, and England torn from the Holy See as a result of Henry VIII's divorce.

Paul III (13 Oct., 1534 – 10 Nov., 1549), Alessandro Farnese, born at Canino 1468. A real statesman, he worked courageously at the reformation of abuses in the Church, called the Council of Trent (1545 – 63) and gave his approbation to the Society of Jesus, 1540. In 1542 he set up the Roman Inquisition at the instance of Carafa who became Paul IV.

Julius III (8 Feb., 1550 – 23 March, 1555), Giovanni Maria Ciocchi del Monte, born in Rome 1487. He had as Papal legate presided over the Council of Trent. He approved the foundation of the German College in Rome, sent Cardinal Pole* to reconcile England to the Church, and empowered him to condone the confiscation of the monastic property by Henry VIII. On 30 Nov., 1554 on the formal petition of both Houses of Parliament, the legate absolved the country from heresy and schism.

Marcellus II (9 April – 1 May, 1555), Marcello Cervini, the last Pope to use his own name; born in 1501 at Montepulciano. " One of the noblest figures in Papal history. " He, Pole and del Monte had been the Legates at the Council of Trent. He was most zealous for the work of reform. All rejoiced at his election, but he died after a reign of three weeks.

Paul IV (23 May, 1555 – 18 Aug., 1559), Giovanni Pietro Carafa. A Neopolitan, born at Capriglio 1476. In concert with St Cajetan he founded the Theatines. Full of zeal for the correction of abuses in the Church, but of ferocious character. He greatly strengthened the action of the Roman Inquisition. He was actuated by a violent hatred of Spanish influence in Italy and an overmastering dread of concessions to the Reformers.

Pius IV (25 Dec., 1559 – 9 Dec., 1565), Gianangelo de' Medici, born at Milan 1499, made his nephew, St Charles Borromeo, Cardinal Secretary of State at the age of 22, reformed abuses in the Sacred College and brought the Council of Trent to a successful conclusion.

St Pius V (8 Jan., 1566 – 1 May, 1572), Michael Ghislieri, a Dominican, made Inquisitor General by Julius III. Published the Roman Catechism, the Breviary, the Missal; established the Congregation of the Index, and formed a victorious league against the Turks (Lepanto 1571). His whole life was devoted to the extirpation of heresy; he was the essence of the Counter-Reformation. He issued the Bull excommunicating and deposing Queen Elizabeth I of England (1570).

Gregory XIII (13 May, 1572 – 10 April, 1585), Ugo Buoncompagni, born at

* Pole had very nearly been elected Pope at the conclave of 1550.

Bologna 1502. He condemned the errors of Baius (1579), reformed the Julian Calendar (1582), founded 23 seminaries, developed the missions and established permanent nunciatures. Between 1558 and 1564 St Philip Neri founded the Congregation of the Oratory in Rome and it was confirmed and approved by Gregory XIII in 1575. A great patron of the new English colleges at Douay and Rome.

Sixtus V (24 April, 1585 – 27 Aug., 1590), Felix Perretti, born 1521, near Montalto, former general of the Franciscans. One of the greatest of the Popes, able and energetic, hard on himself and others. He took very stern measures to restore order in Rome and in the Papal States. He fixed the number of cardinals at 70, reorganized the Roman Curia and the 15 congregations, becoming, thereby, the founder of the modern Papal administrative system.

Urban VII (15 – 27 Sept., 1590). John Baptist Castagna. Of gentle disposition he had been opposed to Sixtus V.

Gregory XIV (5 Dec., 1590 – 15 Oct., 1591), Nicolo Sfondrati, born near Milan, 1535. He encouraged the League in France and excommunicated Henry of Navarre. A great friend of SS Philip Neri and Charles Borromeo.

Innocent IX (29th Oct. – 30 Dec., 1591), John Anthony Facchinetti, of Bologna. Like his predecessor he was greatly under Spanish influence.

Clement VIII (30 Jan., 1592 – 5 March, 1605), Ipollito Aldobrandini, born at Fano, 1536. He was able and energetic, edited the Vulgate, and re-edited the Index (1596). He acknowledged Henry IV as King of France, 1595, when Henry became a Catholic. In 1598 he appointed George Blackwell as ' Archpriest ' in England.

Leo XI (1 – 27 April, 1605), Alessandro de' Medici. As legate to France he had greatly contributed to the settlement of 1595.

Paul V (16 May, 1605 – 28 Jan., 1621), Camillo Borghese, born in Rome 1552. He did much to beautify Rome, and to aid missionary work. He was energetic and capable, but far too favourable to his relations. In this pontificate there was serious trouble with Venice, augmented by Fra Paolo Sarpi. He put an end to the controversy on Divine Grace (*De Auxiliis*) without pronouncing any decision. In 1616 occurred the first censure of Galileo. In 1611 the French Oratory was founded by Cardinal de Bérulle. In 1614 the building of St Peter's was completed.

Gregory XV (9 Feb., 1621 – 8 July, 1623), Alessandro Ludovisi, born at Bologna 1554. A skilled and experienced diplomat. He regulated the Conclave (1621), founded Propaganda (1622), brought back Moravia and Bohemia to the Church, protected the Jesuits and canonized St Ignatius, St Francis Xavier, St Philip Neri, St Teresa of Avila, and others. In 1623 he appointed Dr William Bishop, Vicar Apostolic over England and Scotland, and this form of government continued till 1850.

Urban VIII (6 Aug., 1623 – 29 July, 1644), Maffeo Barberni, born at Florence 1568. Learned, ambitious, and addicted to nepotism. The second condemnation of Galileo by the Inquisition took place in 1633, and the Pope condemned the ' Augustinus ' of Jansenius in 1642. He gave to cardinals and also to the three Ecclesiastical Electors of the Holy Roman Empire the title of " Eminence ". In 1634 the Pope sent Gregorio Panzani to report on the condition of Catholics under Charles I. George Conn was then sent as Papal envoy to Queen Henrietta Maria. On November 18, 1626, Urban consecrated St Peter's. As patron of Bernini he did much to adorn Rome. Supported Richelieu against the Hapsburgs in the Thirty Years' War.

Innocent X (15 Sept., 1644 – 7 Jan., 1655), Giovanni Battista Pamfili, born in Rome 1574. He vainly protested against the articles of the Peace of Westphalia, which laid down the principle that the Prince could choose the religion for his subjects, (Bull *Zelo Domus Dei*, 1648), and condemned the Five Propositions of Jansenius.

Alexander VII (7 April, 1655 – 22 May, 1667), Fabio Chigi, born at Siena 1599. He favoured Spain and Austria and therefore had trouble with Louis XIV. He renewed the condemnation of Jansenius.

Clement IX (20 June, 1667 – 9 Dec., 1669), Giulio Rospigliosi, born at Pistoja 1600. He had been Secretary of State under Alexander VII. He reconciled France and Spain, took great interest in the foreign missions, and forbade missionaries to engage in commerce. He canonized St Peter of Alcantara and St Mary Magdalen de' Pazzi.

Clement X (29 April, 1670 – 22 July, 1676), Emilio Altieri. Born at Rome 1590. Supported the Poles in the struggle with the Turks. He canonized Saints Rose of Lima, Francis Borgia, Cajetan of Thiene, Louis Bertrand, and Philip Benizi.

Blessed Innocent XI (21 Sept., 1676 – 11 Aug., 1689), Benedetto Odescalchi, born at Como 1611, was a saintly reformer who maintained the authority of the Holy See on all occasions, condemned Quietism (1687), reorganized the administration of the Papal States, and fought against nepotism. He appointed four vicars-apostolic for England in 1688, and sent a nuncio to the court of James II. He protested against the Four Articles of Gallican Liberties, 1682. He had much trouble with Louis XIV over the *Droit de regale* and strongly deplored that monarch's persecution of the Huguenots after the Revocation of the Edict of Nantes 1685, but it is not true that he favoured the descent of William of Orange upon England, 1688, to dethrone James II. Beatified 7 October, 1956.

Alexander VIII (6 Oct., 1689 – 1 Feb., 1691), Pietro Ottoboni, born at Venice 1610. He obtained from Louis XIV the restoration of Avignon and Venaissin, but was not deterred from publishing a brief in which he condemned the Four Articles of Gallican Liberties. He was addicted to nepotism. He acquired the books and MSS of Queen Christina of Sweden (1689) for the Vatican Library.

Innocent XII (12 July, 1691 – 27 Sept., 1700), Antonio Pignatelli, born near Naples 1615, obtained from Louis XIV the retraction of the Four Gallican Articles. He condemned Fénelon's book, *The Maxims of the Saints*.

Clement XI (23 Nov., 1700 – 19 March, 1721), Gianfrancesco Albani, born at Urbino 1649. He condemned Jansenism in 1705, and again in 1713 by the Bull *Unigenitus* and pronounced against ' Chinese Rites '.

Innocent XIII (8 May, 1721 – 7 March, 1724), Michelangelo de' Conti, born in Rome 1655. He was obliged to acquiesce in the loss of Parma and Piacenza, assigned to a Spanish Bourbon by the Treaty of Utrecht.

Benedict XIII (27 May, 1724 – 21 Feb., 1730), Pietro Francesco Orsini-Gravina, born at Gravina 1649, a Dominican with a strong interest in the Liturgy and Rubrics. He restored good relations between the Holy See and the Dukes of Sardinia and Savoy, but was less fortunate with Portugal.

Clement XII (12 July, 1730 – 8 Feb., 1740), Lorenzo Corsini, born at Florence 1652, aided the foreign missions, sent the Capuchins to Tibet, condemned the Jansenist Bishop of Utrecht in 1735, and Freemasonry in 1738. A patron of arts and learning, he did much for the improvement of Rome, restored the Arch of Constantine, and erected the Trevi Foundation and the Corsini chapel in St John Lateran.

Benedict XIV (17 Aug., 1740 – 3 May, 1758), Prospero Lambertini, born at Bologna 1675. A celebrated canonist, one of the most learned of the popes, and the ablest between Sixtus V and Leo XIII. He approved the foundation of the Passionists by St Paul of the Cross, 1746, and of the Redemptorists by St Alphonsus Liguori 1749. He founded academies and the Museum of Christian Antiquities in Rome.

Clement XIII (6 July, 1758 – 2 Feb., 1769), Carlo della Torre Rezzonico, born at Venice 1693, he protested against the expulsion of the Jesuits by Pombal (1759) and by the Bourbon Courts, of France (1764), Spain, Naples and Parma (1767). These events caused the death of the Pope.

Clement XIV (19 May, 1769 – 22 Sept., 1774), Giovanni Vicenzo Antonio Ganganelli, born 1705 near Rimini, a Franciscan. Too weak to resist intimidation and the threats of schism, he agreed to suppress the Society of Jesus 1773. It was restored in 1814.

Pius VI (15 Feb., 1775 – 29 Aug., 1799), Giovanni Angelo Braschi, born at Cesena 1717, much troubled by schismatic tendencies in Germany (' Febronianism ') and by State interference, (' Josephism ') in Austria. Went to Vienna, 1782, to appease Joseph II, but with no success. Then the Church in France was almost destroyed by the Revolution (1790 – 97). In 1798 the armies of the French Republic entered Rome, arrested the Pope and deported him to France. He died in captivity at Valence.

Pius VII (14 March, 1800 – 20 Aug., 1823), Luigi Barnabo Chiaramonti, born at Cesena 1742, Bishop of Imola, elected at Venice. He agreed a concordat with Napoleon as First Consul, protesting, however, against the ' Organic Articles ' which had been added to it without having been submitted to him at all. The Pope went to Paris to crown Napoleon as Emperor, 1804, but energetically opposed his overweening pretensions, was arrested (1809) in Rome, and kept a prisoner at Savona and Fontainebleau, re-entered Rome (1814), restored the Society of Jesus (1815). The Papal States were recovered by Cardinal Consalvi at the Congress of Vienna 1815. They had been entirely annexed to the Kingdom of Italy and to the French Empire by Napoleon.

Leo XII (28 Sept., 1823 – 10 Feb., 1829), Annibale della Genga, born at Genga near Spoleto 1760. Reorganized the hierarchy in South America, reconciled many of the schismatical churches in Asia, gave special attention to the national colleges in Rome, made concordats with Switzerland, and the Netherlands, and condemned secret societies. His rigorous and reactionary government of the Papal states bequeathed an insoluble problem to his successors.

Pius VIII (31 March, 1829 – 1 Dec., 1830), Francesco Xaverio Castiglione, born 1761 at Cingoli, in the March of Ancona; issued a brief on mixed marriages in Prussia and denounced Freemasonry. The passing of the Roman

Catholic Emancipation Act took place during the ministry of Sir Robert Peel (1829).

Gregory XVI (2 Feb., 1831 – 1 June, 1846), Bartolommeo Capellari, a Camaldolese monk, born at Belluno, 1765. By military assistance from Austria he secured the maintenance of order in the misgoverned Papal States, where secret societies were ceaselessly at work; he defended the rights of the Church in Prussia and Russian Poland, censured Lamennais in the famous Encyclical *Mirari Vos*. He greatly encouraged foreign missions.

Pius IX (16 June, 1846 – 7 Feb., 1878), Count Giovanni Maria Mastai-Ferreti born at Sinigaglia 1792, was welcomed at his election as a friend of Italian nationalism and liberalism. He was driven from Rome by the revolution in 1848, and returned a conservative. The remaining years of his pontificate saw the steady decline of the Church's temporal power, until Rome itself was occupied by the Piedmontese forces on 20 Sept., 1879. Pius IX defined the doctrine of the Immaculate Conception, 8 Dec., 1854, called the Vatican Council (1869), in which he defined the doctrine of Papal Infallibility, re-established the hierarchy in England (1850), and in Holland (1853).

Leo XIII (20 Feb., 1878 – 20 July, 1903), Gioacchino Vincenzo Raffaele Luigi Pecci, born at Carpineto 1810, one of the greatest statesmen the Church has had, he re-established the prestige of the Holy See in all countries, saw the end of the Kultur-kampf in Germany, and advised French Catholics to rally to the Republic. In 1896 he issued the Bull *Apostolicae Curae*, pronouncing against the validity of Anglican Orders. In masterly encyclicals he dealt with the problems of the time, especially with the Social Question (Encyclical *Rerum novarum*, 1891), and his prestige and influence led to a great spread of the Church in America.

St Pius X (4 Aug., 1903 – 20 Aug., 1914), Giuseppe Melchior Sarto, born at Riese, 2 June, 1835. He greatly promoted Catholic devotion to the Holy Eucharist and reformed the liturgy and the music of the Church. When the Concordat with France was broken (1905), and the Law of Separation (1906) followed, he rejected all offers of the French Government, preferring to retain the liberty of the Church. In 1907 he condemned Modernism. He was beatified by Pope Pius XII in 1951 and canonized in 1954.

Benedict XV (3 Sept., 1914 – 22 Jan., 1922), Giacomo della Chiesa, born at Genoa 1854. He made constant efforts to end the Great War (1914–18) by a negotiated peace, and the rest of his Pontificate was preoccupied with the difficulties of the first years of reconstruction. In 1917 he promulgated a new code of canon law.

Pius XI (6 Feb., 1922 – 10 Feb., 1939), Achille Ratti, born at Desio, near Milan, 31 May, 1857 – " The glorious Pope of the missions ". By the Lateran Treaty, 7 June, 1929, he achieved the creation of the Vatican City as a Sovereign State. A vigorous champion of Christian life and liberty against Nazism, Fascism and Soviet Communism. He canonized Thomas More and John Fisher.

Pius XII (2 Mar., 1939 – 9 Oct., 1958), Eugenio Pacelli, b. Rome, Mar. 2, 1876. A brilliant linguist, he spent 13 years in Germany as Nuncio, first at Munich, then at Berlin (1917 – 1930) when he succeeded Gasparri as Cardinal Secretary of State. He was elected on his 63rd birthday at a single sitting. That Rome emerged unscathed from the Second World War was unanimously ascribed to his action and influence. He defined the Dogma of the Assumption on November 1, 1950. He sanctioned a revision of the Holy Week Liturgy, evening Masses, and a relaxation of the Eucharistic Fast.

John XXIII (28 Oct., 1958 – 3 June, 1963). Angelo Giuseppe Roncalli, b. Sotto il Monte, near Bergamo, Nov. 25, 1881. His simple and informal style produced an immediate change of atmosphere. This was reinforced by his unexpected appearances in the churches and streets of Rome, by visits to hospitals and prisons and in particular by his railway journey to Loreto and Assisi. Early in 1959 came the historic decision to hold the Second Vatican Council with the double object of internal reform and external conciliation, and he created a special Secretariat for the promotion of Christian Unity. The first session of the Council sat from Oct. 11 to December 8, 1962. Very significant were the visits to the Pope of Queen Elizabeth II (May 5, 1961) and of the then Archbishop of Canterbury (Dec. 2, 1960). Among those canonized by Pope John were Martin de Porres and Vincent Pallotti. Powerful Encyclicals such as *Mater et Magistra* (" New Light on Social Problems ") and *Pacem in Terris* (" Peace on Earth "), marked this short but epoch making pontificate.

Paul VI (21 June. 1963 – Aug., 1978), Giovanni Battista Montini, b. Concesio, near Brescia, Sept. 26, 1897, he was elected after a long and distinguished career as a Vatican diplomat.

His early years were preoccupied with the work of the Council begun by his predecessor, and his pontificate as a whole with bringing that work to fruition. All his diplomatic skills were needed to steer the Church through this vital period. Encyclicals such as *Populorum Progressio* and *Ecclesiam Suam* show his concern for social problems and his awareness of the new role of the Church in the modern world, while *Mysterium Fidei* (" The Holy Eucharist "), *Marialis Cultus* (" To Honour Mary "), and, most dramatically, *Humanae Vitae* (" The Regulation of Birth ") show his determination not to compromise its ancient traditions by an uncritical conformity to the spirit of the age. In an eventful period of office, which also saw great strides towards Christian Unity and a successful reform of the Liturgy, Pope Paul also managed to visit the Holy Land, India, Africa and South America. In 1970 he canonised forty of the English Martyrs.

John Paul I (26 Aug., 1978 – 28 Sept., 1978), Albino Luciani, b. Canale d'Agordo, in the Dolomites north of Venice, Oct. 17, 1912. In spite of the shortness of his pontificate—only thirty-three days—his spontaneity, simplicity and holiness have left an indelible impression on the style of the modern papacy.

John Paul II Karol Jozef Wojtyla, b. Wadowice, eighty miles from Krakow, May 18, 1920, elected Pope Oct. 17, 1979.

NOW GLORIOUSLY REIGNING

PUBLISHED BY THE INCORPORATED CATHOLIC TRUTH SOCIETY, LONDON,
AND PRINTED BY THE BURLEIGH PRESS, FISHPONDS, BRISTOL
Printed in England   *July,* 1981
DD